Tl
ABl

and
Promise of God
ISAAC

by Paul Young

OCTOBER 1990
Published by
GOSPEL TRACT PUBLICATIONS
411 Hillington Road, Glasgow G52 4BL, Scotland

ISBN 0 948417 58 7
Copyright ©
GOSPEL TRACT PUBLICATIONS

Printed by
GOSPEL TRACT PUBLICATIONS
411 Hillington Road, Glasgow G52 4BL, Scotland

Contents

Contents

Foreword

The writings of Disraeli, Prime Minister of the last century, advised, "Read no history: nothing but biography, for that is life without theory."

The history of the Bible is essentially the story of its people; men and women of diverse cultures and outlook whose lives were "without theory". Indeed, they were so intensely practical that their lives speak volumes even to this day. As the apostle Paul put it, "All these things happened to them as examples—as object lessons to us—to warn us against doing the same things; they were written down so that we could read about them and learn from them in these last days as the world nears its end." (1 Cor. 10:11, *The Living Bible*).

In this book, Paul Young, a busy itinerant evangelist and elder of a church fellowship in Wales, has diligently researched the biographies of two Bible characters, father and son, Abraham and Isaac. He has ably set their lives in the context of their nation's history but has also identified many practical lessons for Christians of every generation.

This is no dry and academic recital of events in the lives of two great men; its pages certainly enlighten the mind but they also encourage the heart and challenge the will to more holy living. Indeed, the book's devotional emphasis demonstrates unequivocally the writer's principal aim that in the words of Richard of Chichester—readers will "know Jesus Christ more clearly, love him more dearly, follow him more nearly."

Len Davies,
Cardiff, Wales.

Preface

When my wife and I were challenged by the Lord to go out in faith into full-time Christian service, the example of Abraham was used to speak to our hearts. His faith in the living God was both a challenge and an inspiration. He obeyed and God met all his needs, so God has met all our needs in the years since we first obeyed His call.

This book on Abraham and Isaac is the result of studies and sermons preached over many years, and we pray that their wider circulation will prove a blessing to many people.

I am particularly indebted to Len Davies for correcting the original manuscript and writing the foreword. He has been a great source of advice and encouragement.

My thanks also to Gospel Tract Publications for their willingness to publish this book.

Paul Young

ABRAHAM

The Man of Faith

Someone has said that if we need an antidote for the poison of discouragement we should read biographies. Presumably by this he meant that as we read of the ways in which other people have triumphed over difficulties and problems in their lives we will be encouraged to take heart. This, is especially true for Christians who read Biblical biographies, as the triumphs and victories of Bible characters can be ours today, for we serve the same all-powerful God who still longs to work through His people. Also their failures can act as warnings so that we can avoid similar pitfalls in our own lives. Abraham is in both respects a great example for every Christian today.

Abraham's life is one of the best documented in the whole of Scripture. His name appears in at least twenty-seven books of the Bible, although his life's story is mainly told in Genesis chs.11-25. Of Abraham it is written: "He believed God", and as such he is held up in the New Testament as a great example of faith—that faith which is full commitment to God and casts itself upon God for life or death.

In Hebrews 11, where there is that great gallery of Old Testament saints who achieved so much for God by faith, Abraham dominates the chapter. There are more verses devoted to him in this chapter than any other Old Testament character. In the book of Galatians, especially chapters 3 and 4, Abraham is used as an illustration of the Apostle Paul's argument that it is faith and faith alone which is the basis of salvation and acceptance with God. It is significant that Abraham should be so prominent in the Galatian epistle, for that was Martin Luther's favourite Bible book. The man who rediscovered for the Church from the Scriptures the truth of justification by faith, and who was used by God to usher in the Reformation, the good of which we stand in today, was influenced by the experience of Abraham, who knew that message, maybe as long ago as 2,000 years before Christ. For Abraham, all those years before, had been justified by faith.

Abraham is also cited as an example in the Book of Romans, especially in chapter 4, to highlight the truth of justification by faith: "Abraham believed God and it was counted unto him for righteousness" (Romans 4:3). This, of course, is the central message of the Scriptures and of the Gospel of Jesus Christ, that a man is not justified by what he does but by faith in Christ.

It has been rightly said of Abraham that: "He uttered no prophecy, wrote no book, sang no song, gave no laws. Yet in the long line of Bible saints he alone is spoken of as 'the father of the faithful' and as 'the friend of God'." Another has said that: "He is revered by more people than any other man except the Lord Jesus." And that great exception, our Lord Jesus Christ, quoted the example of Abraham to illustrate His teaching while here on earth. The Lord said: "Before Abraham was, I am." In other words He was claiming deity as the God of Abraham. Though Abraham to Jewish eyes was deeply revered—here stood One in the person of Christ who was greater than their father Abraham (see John 8:52-59).

Born in Ur of the Chaldees, Abraham's early name was Abram which means "father of heights". He was the son of Terah and appears to have been born when Terah was 130 years old. However, the Word says: "Now Terah lived seventy years, and begat Abram, Nahor and Haran" (Genesis 11:26). This may seem like a problem but may we suggest that Terah had no children until he was seventy years of age and then he had three sons culminating in Abram 60 years later. This time span would help to explain why Haran died in Ur, the land of his nativity (Genesis 11:28), and left a son Lot, who was comparable in wealth in later years with Abraham and could well have been of similar age. It would therefore seem that in Genesis 11:26 Abram's name appears first in the list of Terah's sons not because of age but because of importance. This means that when Terah died at the age of 205 (Genesis 11:32), Abram would have been 75 years old and that was his age when he departed from Haran (Genesis 12:4). We know he left Haran only after Terah died, for Stephen says: "Then came he (Abram) out of the land of the Chaldïans and dwelt in Charan (Haran); and from thence, **when his father was dead,** he removed him into this land, wherein ye now dwell" (Acts 7:4). This verse clearly states that Abram did not leave Haran until Terah died, and we know that Terah died at the age of 205. Yet Abram left Haran at the age of 75, so simple arithmetic tells us that Abram was born when Terah was 130 years old.

We need never be over anxious about passages of

Scripture which appear contradictory on the surface, and we must never give place to sceptics who claim that there are contradictions in the Word of God. Deeper meditation and conversations with more experienced Christians often bring an answer from the Lord and we must place every confidence in the inspired Word of God.

Ur, Abram's birthplace, was a city dominated by heathendom, sin, idolatry and paganism, yet in the midst of all this God chose and called Abram. God in His sovereignty did not choose Lot, Nahor or even Terah, but he chose Abram. Why Abram? The answer is that we do not know. It maybe that he showed some spiritual qualities the others lacked or had a deeper appreciation of God in worship. Whatever the reason, God called him to leave his country, his kindred and his father's house, and to go to a land that God would show him (Genesis 12:1).

This then was the call to Abram but it took time for him to fully act upon that call from God. When he did eventually act, he went out not from Ur but from Haran, the city to which he had gone with his father. But Abram, believing God, left certainty for uncertainty and the seen for the unseen. Yet he went willingly: "By faith Abraham, when he was called to go out into a place which he should after receive for an inheritance, obeyed and he went out not knowing whither he went" (Hebrews 11:8).

This was a great act of faith. It was a tremendous step into the unknown, which is what faith really is: "Now faith is the substance of things hoped for, the evidence of things not seen" (Hebrews 11:1). Abram was simply taking God at His Word and launching out on His promises. ⌉He had to leave Mesopotamia with its culture, wealth and security. He had to leave home, family and friends. He had to make detailed arrangements for the journey. He had to embark upon a trip which could prove dangerous and could put him and his family in jeopardy. He had to go out not knowing the final destination. We can imagine him facing the tears, the heartache and the wrench of departure. He had to go and know that he would never return. But why did he go? He went because God had said to go and he chose to obey God. He went because God had promised him blessings and Abram wanted God's blessing.

What a man of faith! No wonder he is called the father of the faithful. It is as if he said: "God, I trust You completely. Lord, I will follow You to the ends of the earth, if You want me to".

God had made a threefold promise to Abram: a land would be given, as would a multitude of descendants, and thirdly there was a spiritual promise: "and in thee shall all families of the earth be blessed" (Genesis 12:1-3). The land was Canaan. The descendants were the children of Israel, who through the ages have been as "the stars in heaven" (Genesis 15:5) and as "the dust of the earth" (Genesis 13:16), too many to count. This was a promise in spite of the barrenness of Sarah's womb. Later Abram's name was changed to Abraham (Genesis 17:5) which means "a father of a multitude". Finally, the spiritual promise was fulfilled in the person of the Lord Jesus Christ, the greatest descendant of Abraham. So on the strength of these promises Abram left Haran and went out to places unknown.

How many Christians today would, despite all God's promises, exercise such faith? We took that first step into the unknown when we trusted Christ for salvation and committed ourselves to Him, but He has also called us to service. The moment we availed ourselves of His invitation to "come" (Matthew 11:28), was also the moment He said "go". "Go ye therefore, and teach all nations, . . . and, lo, I am with you alway, . . . "(Matthew 28:19-20). This is a commission to all believers. Do we in faith fulfil this commandment?

The apostle Paul a descendant of Abraham was on a ship which was being battered by the waves of a fierce storm in the Mediterranean Sea and still he could say: "Sirs, I believe God"(Acts 27:25). Yet who will rise up in our country today as we see it battered by the storm waves of spiritual decline and moral pollution, and say "I believe God"? Who will trust God for our country, our city, our town or street, or even our family? Abraham was able to trust God over 4,000 years ago, and the apostle Paul also in his day, in spite of difficult circumstances. We can also thank God for the men of faith who, through the ages and even into our own generation, have captured something of the faith that motivated Abram those years ago.

William Booth is one such example who saw the gin parlours, the prostitution and filthy, dirty children in the streets of industrial London and found his destiny in seeking to help them. He assembled a salvation army who would go out in faith and kneel in the centre of British towns and claim those towns for God. They took a courageous stand and ran the gauntlet of jeering crowds who spat at them and threw dead animals. Yet they prayed, preached the Word of God and helped the poor, for they had caught something of the great faith which motivated the heart of Abram. They did a tremendous amount to relieve the spiritual and physical suffering of many people in 19th century Britain.

In the 1950's a young preacher in Pennsylvania was so moved by God as he saw the face of a young murderer in 'Life' magazine, that he went out in faith to be God's witness amongst the tenements of New York City and founded 'Teen Challenge'. That utter obedience to God in faith has been the means of saving many who were caught in the clutches of Satan through violence and drug abuse. David Wilkerson tells his story in *The Cross and the Switchblade*.

Do you sense the call of God in your heart? Are you being challenged by God 'to go'? It may be to a specific sphere of service or it may be a more general call to serve and witness. It may be to a quiet work: visiting the sick, the old, the bereaved or the lonely, to help, comfort and witness to them. It may be to start or to assist in running a Christian Fellowship in your place of work, school or college. It may be to talk to friends and family about the Lord. It may be to become more actively involved in the local church. What is your response? Will you question God and produce all sorts of excuses as Moses did when God called him (Exodus chs.3 and 4)? Will you run away from situations and opportunities like Jonah did when God called him (Jonah 1)? Will you doubt God's call as Thomas doubted that Jesus was risen from the dead (John 20:24-25)? God tells us to listen, to trust and to go out on His promises and see Him work in mighty ways.

That was Abram's experience. His first great act of faith was to go "not knowing whither he went". His faith however went further than that, for he really believed that God would fulfil His promise and give him a son. This was in spite of a considerable delay, for it was 25 years after leaving Haran, when Abraham was 100 years old, that the promise was fulfilled (Genesis 21:5). We can imagine the temptation through those years of waiting to doubt, to distrust God or to think that God had forgotten His promise. Yet through it all Abraham had a living, active, working faith in God. His faith overcame the improbable human circumstances of Sarah's barrenness and the fact that she was past the normal age when women bear children. It seemed almost as if Abraham knew the words of the Lord Jesus: "With men it is impossible, but not with God: for with God all things are possible" (Mark 10:27). Do we believe, as we think of our unsaved friends and relatives? Do we believe, when we think of the morally impoverished state of our nation? Do we believe, when we consider the hardness of Islam or the difficulties in Communist lands? Do we really believe that God can still work in our day? He can!

It is too easy to become discouraged, to feel that the situation is hopeless and that God will never work. But as I write this I am reminded of the verse: "Pray without ceasing" (1 Thessalonians 5:17) and of a lady who did just that and saw God work in a wonderful way. For over 30 years that lady prayed many times each day for the conversion of her only son. She never gave up even though for a long time there was a total lack of spiritual interest on his part. Eventually, her faith and persistence were rewarded, and I could sense her joy as she wrote to me one day to say that her son had openly confessed Christ as his Saviour. At times, as with Abraham, we must hold on to God's promises, trusting completely in Him and believing that He and He alone has called us.

It is Abraham's faith as he remembers and clings to God's promises that shines through his trials. He had to wait patiently for the fulfilment of God's personal promise to him and it almost seems that the greater the faith, the greater the trials, but eventually the waiting was over and we read those joyful words: "Sarah conceived and bare Abraham a son in his old age" (Genesis 21:2).

Yet, even with this longed-for son came more trials, for in Genesis 22 we hear God saying to Abraham: "Offer Isaac for a burnt offering". We can imagine the thoughts that might have raced through Abraham's mind, yet there was no hesitation. "Yes, Lord, I'll give you my only son," he seemed to say. He could not understand it but nothing was going to come between Abraham and his Lord, not even the most precious thing in his life—Isaac his son. In this way Abraham becomes a type of God the Father who offered up His Son on Calvary's cross for our sins. "By faith Abraham, when he was tried, offered up Isaac: and he that had received the promises offered up his only begotten son, Of whom it was said, That in Isaac shall thy seed be called. Accounting that God was able to raise him up, even from the dead; from whence also he received him in a figure" (Hebrews 11:17-19). Of course it was not Isaac's life which God desired, it was Abraham's heart. Abraham did not fail, for he was willing to give to God his precious son. In effect he said: "Lord, take everything". In Abraham's life there was no idol, nothing to break communion with God, and this was so openly demonstrated on Mount Moriah. This then, was Abraham's faith—total commitment of all he had to God.

God still calls His people to 100% devotion to
Himself. As Christians today, we should not allow
anything—a relationship, activity, ambition, money or
whatever, to come between us and God. He should be
of the greatest importance and preciousness to us. Are
we not commanded to love Him with all our heart, with
all our soul, with all our strength and with all our mind?
(Luke 10:27). This was Abraham's devotion towards
God, and as such he is called: "the friend of God" (2
Chronicles 20:7 and James 2:23). The Lord Jesus says
to Christians today: "Ye are my friends, if ye do
whatsoever I command you" (John 15:14). Is this our
kind of faith, that we trust Him so much that whatever
He commands us we do, and so become His friends?
This was certainly the faith of Abraham, as we have
seen. We would do well to try to follow in the footsteps
of faithful Abraham, remembering that without faith it
is impossible to please God (Hebrews 11:6).

> But we never can prove
> The delights of His love,
> Until all on the altar we lay;
> For the favour He shows,
> And the joy He bestows,
> Are for them who will trust and obey.
> *(John Henry Sammis)*

This first section has been about the faith of
Abraham, and God in His grace draws only this aspect
of the man to our attention in Hebrews 11. Yet
Abraham was subject to dreadful failure and great fears.
Thus he failed, but rose up in faith to overcome failure
by the power of God.

The Man of Failure

In introducing this section in the life of Abraham, another Old Testament character springs readily to mind, namely, Elijah. He had first-hand knowledge of the power of God and saw God triumph in a wonderful way on Mount Carmel (1 Kings 18), yet we read that he was "a man subject to like passions as we are" (James 5:17), and he also knew defeat, despair and the desire to give up in depression, even though he was a great man of God.

Similarly Abraham, although a great man of faith and wonderfully commended for his faith throughout Scripture, also knew very grave failure in his spiritual life. Some of his failures have had dire consequences, the effects of which we still feel today. Thus he was both a man of faith and a man of failure. We need to imitate the faith of Abraham, but as we look at the times when he failed God, we should take note and try to avoid similar pitfalls. It is essentially an example of what not to do.

It is the revelation of all the varied aspects of the men of God which makes the Bible both credible and creditable. It is this dwelling upon both the failures and triumphs of God's men which lifts the Scriptures above the level of myth or mere story. There is a ring of reality and truthfulness to the stories and biographies of men and women in Scripture for their problems and defeats are not glossed over. All great men of God have had their weaknesses and their areas of failure. Only One is perfect and without sin, that is God's Son: the Lord Jesus Christ (see Hebrews 7:26; 1 Peter 2:21-22; and Luke 23:14-15). Christ has no rivals in holiness and purity, for He had no weakness or area of failure.

The fact that Abraham conquered his failures through faith, is the key to why his faith is held up as such a great example. When Abraham failed he did not remain in a failed or defeated condition—faith triumphed.

There were three areas of failure in the life of Abraham:

a. In relationship to his father Terah.
b. In relationship to his nephew Lot.
c. In relationship to his wife Sarai.

a. Failure in relationship to Terah

"Now the Lord had said unto Abram, Get thee out of thy country, and from thy kindred, and from thy father's house, unto a land that I will shew thee" (Genesis 12:1). This is a reminder of something God had said earlier. When Abram was in Ur of the Chaldees, he had been called by God to go to a land that God would show him. Yet Abram failed to go, at least initially he failed to go.

Even though the call had been to Abram, it appears that Terah was still very much in control of the family group, for it was Terah who led them northwards to Haran. In other words, Abram, instead of instantly obeying the voice of God and cutting loose from family and friends, delayed and allowed himself to be led by his father to Haran. Here he was still in Mesopotamia, still in the same culture from which he had been called, with its familiar ways and customs. At this stage he was not a pilgrim for God, nor a stranger in this world.

Abram's failure to act instantly in obedience caused a delay in departure, which may have been as much as 15 years. Thus 15 years were wasted which could have been used in service for God. Abram had made a partial break and no doubt he had encouraged Terah to leave the city of Ur, but he failed to make a complete break until Terah had died. Thus he waited until human circumstances seemed right, and only then did he launch out in faith claiming the promises of God. In other words, Abram had a call, but only partially obeyed it when he departed with Terah to Haran.

There is similarity here with Ananias and his wife Sapphira in the early church (Acts 5:1-11). They knew the call of God to lay all before Him and yet when they sold land they only pretended they had given all the money thus obtained to God. In fact they kept some back for themselves, for they still harboured the desire for worldly wealth. God slew them for their lies, as a warning to other believers. Later on in the book of Acts we read of the young man John Mark who set out with Barnabas and Paul on the first missionary journey, yet sadly: "they came to Perga in Pamphylia: and John departing from them returned to Jerusalem" (Acts 13:13). This was failure on the part of John, who had heard the call but had not fully committed himself to the Lord's work, and so gave up. It is a poor sense of calling if we go only part way for God.

God still calls every Christian to full commitment to Himself, and we must ask ourselves the question "Have we truly cut loose from the world, or are we still dominated by ambition and the desire to accumulate worldly possessions?" It is a sad experience in life to talk to born again believers whose conversation rarely has anything whatever to do with the Lord or with spiritual things, but everything to do with worldliness and the

latest addition to material well-being. What dominates
our conversation, our talk, our thoughts, our minds? Is
it the Lord? It should be.

Have we cut clean away in repentance from our old
lives? Is there a marked difference between what we
were before we trusted Christ and what we are in
Christ? There should be a real distinction between the
non-Christian who considers this life his home and the
Christian who is a pilgrim and a stranger in this world,
looking forward to his home in Heaven. It took years
for Abram to cut loose completely and become a
pilgrim for God. Let us not waste precious time
following our own inclinations and desires but may we
give ourselves in obedience to God's will for our lives
without delay.

b.   Failure in relationship to Lot

Lot was the skeleton in Abraham's cupboard. What
we mean by the term "skeleton in the cupboard" is that
there is something in our lives or background of which
we are ashamed, so we never mention it and keep it a
well guarded secret. Unfortunately such skeletons have
a habit of surfacing at most embarrassing times. It is
only when the room is full of people that the cupboard
door unexpectedly swings open to reveal the skeleton
within. This turned out to be so true in the experience
of Abraham.

God, when He revealed His perfect will to Abram had
said that he must leave his country, kindred and father's
house (Genesis 12:1). In other words Abram's call was
to separate himself from his homeland and his relatives.
This may seem a little hard, even a harsh thing for a
loving God to say to His servant. But God knows

everything and He knew that Terah and then Lot would ultimately divert Abram from His will and purpose and would ruin his testimony before the heathen. This is similar to the very strict rules which the children of Israel were given about not allowing their sons and daughters to marry the heathen (Deuteronomy 7:3). God knew that foreign partners would lead His people into the practice of idolatry, as indeed did happen, when Israel disobeyed these rules.

Abram would have been spared many problems had he completely obeyed God. His action in taking Lot with him may have been understandable from a human point of view, and was perhaps based upon selfish reasons and feelings of insecurity, but he had to learn the hard way (as we do sometimes) that God's way is always best.

It is sad to read: "And there was a strife between the herdmen of Abram's cattle and the herdmen of Lot's cattle: and the Canaanite and the Perizzite dwelled then in the land" (Genesis 13:7). Why is our attention drawn to the fact that these heathen nations lived in the land at that time? Surely, this is something we already knew. Yet the Spirit of God emphasises it to us because the cupboard door had swung open just as these heathen nations were gazing on. Abram's disobedience had led to a poor testimony in front of the heathen. They could see quarrel and strife among the people of God. This would not have happened had Abram fully submitted himself to God's instructions and left Lot behind. Disobedience by Abram lowered the majesty of God in the eyes of these heathen. We must take warning for our disobedience can also lead to a weakened testimony, and unfortunately this is all too true of many local churches. Strife has developed. Quarrels (howbeit very often covert ones) are allowed to fester for years, and so blessing, joy and true fellowship are withheld from the people of God. No wonder the unsaved in many areas are largely untouched by Christian witness. We need to put our own houses in order before effective testimony and outreach are achieved towards the unsaved. We need to take to heart the words of the Apostle Paul: "Forbearing one another, and forgiving one another, if any man have a quarrel against any: even as Christ forgave you, so also do ye" (Colossians 3:13). It is in this way we should put matters right.

Abram had to put the matter right and end the strife between the respective herdmen, and so with commendable lack of selfishness, he desires peace and unity by giving Lot the choice of direction in departing. " . . . separate thyself, I pray thee, from me: if thou wilt take the left hand, then I will go to the right; or if thou depart to the right hand, then I will go to the left" (Genesis 13:9). So Lot went in the direction of the well-watered plains, to human eyes the best land. At last Abraham had completely cut loose from his kindred.

When Lot had gone God again revealed himself to Abraham. This time He tells Abram to look out on all the land, for one day all that he can see will he his (Genesis 13:14-15). It is interesting to note that Abraham's first vision from God was in Ur (Genesis 12:1), his second came when he had broken away from Haran and had gone out not knowing whither he went (Genesis 12:7). In other words not until he had left his father's house in response to the first vision did he receive a second. His third came "after that Lot was separated from him" (Genesis 13:14).

There is a progression here. As Abraham surrendered to God's will—so God blessed him. With every step of obedience to God's revealed will came more light. God revealed more of His will to Abram, only when Abram heeded and obeyed what He had said in previous visions. Obedience to God's revealed will must be the hallmark of every believer. It is wonderful to know that as God had a purpose and a plan for Abram's life, so He has for us and it is exciting to find out that purpose as we go a step at a time with God.

So Lot was Abram's skeleton in the cupboard. The door had swung open just as heathen, idol worshipping eyes were on the cupboard door. Any Christian may have a skeleton, such as a past sin, or action, or relationship, it may even be something that continues. One may be even reaping its effects today. I know a preacher who is used by God to great effect—yet he is in constant pain due to a heart condition, caused through heavy drinking in pre-conversion days. He is reaping the effects of pre-conversion sins in post-conversion days. God has forgiven him and is greatly using him, but nature can't forgive Him. " ... whatsoever a man soweth, that shall he also reap" (Galatians 6:7).

The Apostle Paul had something of a skeleton in the cupboard, which could be used by the Judaisers of his day, for he had persecuted the church of Jesus Christ. But Paul's answer simply was this: "Forgetting those things which are behind and reaching forth unto those things which are before, I press toward the mark for the prize of the high calling of God in Christ Jesus" (Philippians 3:13-14). That is exactly what Abraham did, like Paul he did not dwell upon past failures, but rose up and conquered them through faith in God.

It is not good for Christians to dwell upon past failure, but we must press on in faith and have confidence in God. We must really accept the fact that God has cleansed and forgiven us, and to remember that: "There is therefore now no condemnation to them which are in Christ Jesus" (Romans 8:1). Yet if we have a problem, a continuing area of failure or a genuine skeleton in the cupboard; for example, a harbouring up of resentment, bitterness or hatred towards someone else, what do we do?

We need to remember that God has already forgiven us and no longer condemns us. Yet His fellowship with us may be distant because of this continuing sin. We need to confess our sins to Him, "If we confess our sins he is faithful and just to forgive us our sins and to cleanse us from all unrighteousness" (1 John 1:9). This was written to Christians so that fellowship with God can be renewed. God wants to renew fellowship, and as soon as we have in repentance confessed, He says in effect: "Forget it and press on". Maybe too we need to seek the forgiveness of others and put matters right. This is certainly not easy, but it has to be done to avoid matters simmering for years and producing divided situations like that for example at the church in Corinth (see 1 Corinthians 3:3-5; 11:18).

Also we need to renew our minds daily in the Scriptures (Romans 12:2). This helps us keep the mind clean and pure. This is well illustrated in the story of a young Christian who read his Bible often, but seemed to understand and retain so little of what he read. He went to an older Christian and complained that his Bible readings were a thorough waste of time, as he retained so little of what he read. The older Christian said: "Is it any use to pour water into a sieve?" "No," was the reply. Yet, as was then pointed out, it is useful, for running water keeps the sieve clean. Likewise, if we constantly read and meditate upon the Word of God it will keep our minds clean and enable us to live lives which will not produce skeletons in the cupboard. Abram ultimately became free from skeletons in the cupboard and found power in testimony before the heathen by living wholeheartedly for God.

c. Failure in relationship to Sarai

In Genesis 15:4 God had again visited Abram and had confirmed that "out of thine own bowels shall be thine heir." God's presence in the smoking furnace and the burning lamp confirmed the promise by moving among the carcases of dead animals laid out on the ground to seal the covenant (Genesis 15:8-18).

So in chapter 16 Abram knew that he was going to have a son to be his heir. Up to this time he had been faithful to one wife namely: Sarai. It seems that there was no direct word from the Lord that the heir would be Sarai's son—this was assumed. Yet we can imagine Abram pondering how an heir would be provided. How would God do it? Especially as Sarai was so old and so barren. It all seemed so impossible. Thus when Sarai mentions a plan we can imagine why Abram seized upon it so eagerly. He wanted God's promise to be fulfilled, but he thought that he could help out and do things in human strength. His motive may have been good but his actions were wrong. Abram hardly waited to think and so failed to notice the three things which were wrong with Sarai's plan.

Firstly, Abram accepted Sarai's argument as valid.

She instigated the plan and even couched her words in religious terms—it sounded plausible. "And Sarai said unto Abram, Behold now, **the Lord** hath restrained me from bearing: I pray thee, go in unto my maid; it maybe that I may obtain children by her. And Abram hearkened to the voice of Sarai" (Genesis 16:2). What a pity that Abram listened to the voice of his wife, for she led him into the way of failure. The plan sounded as if it had God's seal of approval upon it, yet even if it was true that the Lord had restrained her from child-bearing, surely God in His power could reverse the process. Abram didn't ask, and in accepting the plan as valid he accepted Sarai's rather faulty spiritual logic.

Secondly, in accepting the plan and putting it into operation Abram was imitating the common practice of pagan society of those days. It was usual for a servant girl to produce children and raise them up in the name of a barren mistress. So Abram copied the heathen practices of those around and compromised his position of trusting God and his commitment to one woman—which is always God's way (see Hebrews 13:4; Genesis 2:24). This is a great lesson for us to learn, that nothing is ever achieved for the Lord through compromises with and imitation of the world.

Thirdly, Abram did not consult God on the matter. There was no recourse to prayer. There was no seeking the mind of God, instead he went straight ahead and fulfilled the plan. Unfortunately, many Christians today are in no position to criticise for is it not true that in many Christian activities there is far too much discussion, argument and consultation, and far too little prayer. We talk with many people about many things instead of talking it over with our Heavenly Father. Five minutes of prayer is worth hours of discussion. Let us not continue in this neglect of prayer.

So, as a result of this failure Ishmael was born to Hagar the Egyptian bondservant. Sadly, there were unfortunate results from Abraham's failure.

Firstly, Hagar became proud and arrogant especially towards Sarai, for "her mistress was despised in her eyes" (Genesis 16:4). The wise man knew what he meant when he said: "For three things the earth is disquieted and for four which it cannot bear; For a servant when he reigneth; and a fool when he is filled with meat; For an odious woman when she is married; **and an handmaid that is heir to her mistress"** (Proverbs 30:21-23). This was certainly seen in the reaction of Hagar to Sarai.

Secondly, Sarai became bitter and resentful both towards Hagar and towards Abram. She complained to Abram about Hagar's attitude and he in effect said: "she's yours, do what you like to her". So pregnant Hagar fled away because Sarai started to ill-treat her. But God sent her back to her mistress with the promise that her son would also become a great nation (Genesis 16:6-14). So Abram had a household riddled with tension, division and antagonism, all due to his compromise and his failure to consult God.

Finally, through the ages the descendants of Ishmael—the Arabs—have been antagonistic towards the descendants of Isaac—the Jews—and vice versa. Even into our own day we have seen wars and continuing tensions and fearful consequences for world peace emanating from the Middle East, due to Abram's sin. We all live in a tense and divided world caused in part at least by the actions of this one man.

It is true as Abram found out that we cannot sin with impunity. Compromise in spiritual things never succeeds. We must never as Christians take matters into our own hands—without consulting God and His Word. We must be wary of quick, snap decisions and also take care that those who are close to us do not lead us astray, even unwittingly. We must work out the principles for Christian behaviour from the Scriptures through regularly reading and studying the Bible.

Yet we can take encouragement that in spite of Abraham's failure he is held up as a model of faith. Thus when we fail the Lord, and we do all too often, He says: "Don't remain a failure". God has called us to triumph and victory in spiritual things. Each believer has a real part to play in the overall great victory of God. We thus must be like Abraham and not remain guilt-ridden, defeated, mediocre and failed, but we must rise up in confession, repentance and faith. Only then will we like Abraham know God's power and victory in our lives.

The Man of Fears

At some time or another fear afflicts us all. It is universal in its effect. It can cause us to freeze into inaction, to act irrationally, or even cause us to go against our principles and fail God. We feel so guilty afterwards and wish that we had not behaved in such a cowardly manner.

Yet not all fear is bad. There is in all of us an instinctive fear in the presence of immediate danger. I well remember as a little boy in South Wales, walking home across a field, and suddenly seeing a movement in the grass. I saw what I thought was a snake and removed myself rather hurriedly with fear-induced speed. In hindsight the creature turned out to be a harmless slow worm. But I knew fear. That sort of fear is a God-implanted mechanism which produces fear in the face of danger and is useful for self-preservation. This is God-given fear which generates caution.

There are however fears which are not good, and even legitimate fears when carried too far can become phobias or compulsive fears of imagined danger. I know a lady who suffers from claustrophobia which is: "a morbid dread of confined areas" (*The Concise Oxford Dictionary*). I suffer a little bit from acrophobia which is: "a morbid dread of heights" (*The Concise Oxford Dictionary*). Yet it is too easy to suffer from other fears such as: a fear of being criticised, or of being ridiculed, or of suffering financial loss. If these sorts of fears are allowed to remain we will do very little service for God.

Abraham's fear was that of violent death at the hands of men who wanted his attractive wife Sarah for themselves. This fear caused Abraham to lie, to deceive and to encourage adultery on the part of others, not to mention the possible violation of Sarah's integrity. It also made him act faithlessly towards God.

Thus induced by fear, Abraham concocted a scheme which he felt would save his life. The scheme was that if anyone was attracted to, Sarah, she would say that she was his sister and not mention that fact that she was his wife. Thus Abraham deduced that he would not be killed and might even be greatly honoured for the sake of Sarah. On two occasions he put his little scheme into action.

The first occasion is recorded in Genesis 12:9-20. There was a famine in the land of Canaan. So Abram went into Egypt for food and realised that the practice of the day was often to kill a husband so that the attractive wife could be taken. Thus he pretended to be the brother of Sarai. Now his words contained some truth for she was his half-sister (their father was the same, but they had different mothers see Genesis 20:12). But he meant the words as lies. He was in effect saying she is my sister and NOT my wife.

We must notice what Abram did wrong. Firstly, he failed to consult with God about providing food for them in Canaan, and about the necessity to go into Egypt. Secondly, he failed to trust in God for protection, and failed to remember God's promise. Thirdly, he resorted to man-made schemes of lying and deceiving.

The fear of being murdered had caused Abram to forget God and to act in a fleshly way rather than a spiritual way. The results were a plague on Egypt, and Abram together with Sarai were sent back to Canaan by Pharaoh. Also they had left a poor testimony before the heathen; yet Abram was enriched, for Pharaoh had bestowed much wealth upon him, which he was allowed to keep. God had caused Abram's sin to produce material blessing from Pharaoh, king of Egypt. It was almost as if God was saying: "I'll make you great in spite of your sin".

The second occasion the scheme went into operation was among the people who dwelt in Gerar (Genesis 20:1-18). Again God was not consulted, again a plague came, this time upon the household of the ruler Abimelech (who had taken Sarah into his harem). Amazingly God visited Abimelech in a dream by night, for this man it would seem knew God. So the matter had to be righted and Sarah returned to Abraham.

In both cases Sarah was kept by God from heathen defilement. In both cases too Abraham acted completely out of character because of fear. Yet God would have strengthened him and put some backbone into him, if only he had come wholeheartedly before the Lord in devotion. The Lord can strengthen the weak and make the coward brave.

Years later Queen Esther, a descendant of Abraham, had to conquer her fear through the power of God, as she went before King Ahasuerus saying: "If I perish, I perish" (Esther 4:16). It was a courageous act to come before the king unbidden, but she did it. She had given over her life completely to God in faith and so was enabled to conquer her fear and ultimately save her people from annihilation.

Even later we find the Apostle Peter defeated, as his courage had shrivelled and he denied the Lord with swearing and cursing (Mark 14:66-72). But he conquered his fear through repenting and by trusting fully in the risen Christ. In the book of the Acts he could go out and preach to huge crowds and stand boldly before the leaders of his day and proclaim God's message (Acts 2:14-40; 4:5-21). In the Acts it is Peter's boldness which stands out; his fear was conquered by full surrender to Christ.

Fear is an enemy of us all. The courageous man or woman is NOT the one who does not know fear, but the one who conquers it. That is why the Bible mentions so ofen the phrase: "Fear not". Some one has said that there are as many 'fear nots' in the Bible as days in the year. God in His wisdom and mercy has given us a "Fear not" for every day of the year. Indeed, God's answer to

Abram was: "Fear not, Abram: I am thy shield and thy exceeding great reward" (Genesis 15:1).

We may be all too often immobilised in our witness because of fear, and we may bear, like Abraham, a poor testimony for God. Young people especially have fears such as: seeming to be different from others, of having to go against the crowd, of being out in the cold socially, of being ridiculed. Many in all age groups are afraid of the unknown in door to door work, or of abuse and difficult questions they might get when they witness. These are areas where we all tend to get fears. One dear brother once prayed: "Lord we are shaking in our shoes at the prospect of door to door evangelism". Yet God says to us: "Fear not". We can only conquer fear by trusting God and believing His promise: "Lo I am with you alway" (Matthew 28:20).

We can take a number of warnings from Abraham. Firstly, Abraham failed to pray and so found himself engulfed by fear. Thus we must always consult God in prayer. We can take all, literally everything to God in prayer. We have heard it said that the power house of the local church is the prayer meeting. That is true, yet why is it the most poorly attended meeting each week in many churches? On the wall of the room, where for a number of years I taught a weekly Bible Class, is a poster which says: "Things go better with prayer". Yet it seems to me that we have lost so much in Christian circles because we fail to really get down to prayer. Someone has said that in the church today we want more pray-ers and less pay-ers. We really need to learn to agonize in prayer for the power to overcome fear.

> Are we weak and heavy laden,
> Cumber'd with a load of care?

Precious Saviour, still our refuge
Take it to the Lord in prayer.
(Joseph Scriven)

Secondly, Abraham failed to be obedient to God, thus we must always be obedient. Unlike Abraham we must never resort to lies and deceit, never mind how costly the path of honesty and obedience may appear to be. So we should be obedient to the Lord's universal commandment to believers: "Go ye into all the world, and preach the Gospel" (Mark 16:15). Let us overcome fear and obey this commandment of the Lord, daily in our lives.

Finally, we need to always remember God's promise: Abraham in his fear forgot. We in our fear may forget the promise: "... I am with you alway" (Matthew 28:20). When we go and testify He will always be with us—to strengthen, guide and give us power. Let us rely upon that divine power and know Him at work in our witness. It is beneficial to read books, articles and courses on personal evangelism, but we can really only learn the art of personal evangelism by doing it. We must not submit to the fear which leaves us immoblised in personal evangelism. Instead we need to rise up in faith on the promises of God. We need to surrender our pride, our standing, our ambition and give them up and go all out in service for God.

We must imitate the faith of Abraham, so that we can rise above failure and overcome fear. Let us like Abraham learn to live in the power of the Lord, and be continually filled with joy as we live victoriously in Christ.

ISAAC

Isaac stands second in line of the three founding fathers of Israel. He succeeds Abraham His father, but precedes his son Jacob. His name appears in at least twenty-one books of the Bible, usually in a list with the other two patriarchs. The Lord Jesus, referring back to the book of Moses, quoted: "I am the God of Abraham, and the God of Isaac, and the God of Jacob" (Mark 12:26). This is repeated frequently in the Scriptures.

Abraham was a strong, powerful and much respected man in the land of Canaan, and the Lord was his God. Jacob was ruthlessly cunning and achieved both a large family and great wealth largely through guile. God was even the God of Jacob the repentant deceiver. However, Isaac, as we shall see, was altogether different. He was weak and possessed neither the drive of Abraham nor the guile of Jacob. Yet we read that God was the God of Isaac too. Such truths give us much encouragement, for whatever type of character we possess God wants to be and will be our God, if we let Him. He does not only accept those who have attractive personalities, but also those who are weak by nature. In fact He will accept anyone who calls upon Him in faith (John 3:16).

Abraham and Jacob did not live as long as Isaac, who lived to be one hundred and eighty years old (Genesis 35:28), yet much less is recorded of Isaac's life than that of either Abraham or Jacob. His life seems to have created little impact either with men or God—for Isaac had fewer communications from the Lord than either of the other two. Abraham received eight communications (Genesis 12:1-3; 12:7; 13:14-17; 15:1-21; 17:1-22; 18:1-33; 21:12-13 and also his time of testing Genesis 22). Jacob received six (Genesis 28:12-15; 31:3; 32:24-29; 35:9-13; 46:2-4; also 32:2). Isaac received only two (Genesis 26:2-5; 26:24). His life story is mainly told in Genesis chs.21-35, though only chapter 26 is solely devoted to him. However, we can build up a picture of this man's life and character. Again, as with Abraham, there are pitfalls in his life which are recorded for our warning but there are good points which we must seek to imitate.

The apostle Paul uses Isaac as an allegory of the new covenant (Galatians 4:22-31). Paul talks of Abraham's two sons: one was born to the bondwoman Hagar (Genesis 16:15), and the other was born to the freewoman Sarah (Genesis 21:2). The former was Ishmael, the latter Isaac. Ishmael represents the law (old covenant) which leads to bondage, while Isaac represents the new covenant in Christ which engenders freedom. The answer to this conflict was to cast out the bondwoman for she was not to be heir with the free (Genesis 21:14). Paul was using this to illustrate the argument that the Galatians should dispense with legalism and be content with faith in Christ as the sole criterion for salvation. Like Isaac, believers "are the children of promise . . . not children of the bondwoman but of the free" (Galatians 4:28 and 31). Thus the Christian is not under the bondage of the law.

"Free from the law, oh wondrous condition,
Jesus has died and there is remission".

On the whole Isaac's life was undistinguished, almost colourless. He lacked the great energy and initiative which so clearly characterised Abraham and Jacob. Someone has described him as "the ordinary son of a great father, and the ordinary father of a great son". He has also been described as a noble son, a faithful husband and a weak father. Yet there was much about his life which pleased God. We will view the life of Isaac in three ways:

1. The Promised Life
2. The Passive Life
3. The Prayer Life.

1. The Promised Life

"...but he (who was) of the freewoman was by promise" (Galatians 4:23).

Here Isaac is a type of Christ, for both had births which were foretold years before the actual event. In the case of Christ, those prophecies were made hundreds of years prior to His birth (Micah 5:2; Isaiah 7:14), and were given in detail. They were also fulfilled to the letter in remarkable ways. In the case of Isaac the time span between prophecy and event, although much less, was nevertheless significant.

Initially, the promise was given in Genesis chapter 12, when Abram was still in Ur of the Chaldees. But it was twenty five years after leaving Haran that God gave him Isaac. The time span between initial promise and ultimate fulfilment could thus have been as much as forty years.

Not only was Isaac's birth prophesied, but it was also miraculous. Abraham by then was one hundred years old and Sarah over ninety. She was far past the age when women normally give birth to children, yet God gave her a son in her old age. Her life became filled with joy and laughter, and her heart was able to rejoice. That is why his name was Isaac. Isaac means "he laugheth" or "laughing one". Certainly his birth caused great delight, but it also takes us back to two prophecies concerning the birth of Isaac. When God had reiterated His promise to Abraham that a son would be born to Sarah (Genesis 17:15-19), Abraham laughed. His laughter was questioning laughter: "And shall Sarah that is ninety years old bear?" (Genesis 17:17). Later God returned to the subject of the promise and Sarah was in the tent listening (Genesis 18:9-15). God said: "And, lo, Sarah thy wife shall have a son". Sarah inwardly laughed at such a suggestion for she found it very hard to believe. Yet the parents' laughter, which had been questioning and incredulous in the past, was turned into genuine joy as God fulfilled his promise with the birth of Isaac.

In his miraculous birth Isaac is again seen as a type of Christ, who also had a miraculous birth. The difference was that He was not born of an old woman but to a young woman—a virgin (Luke 1:30-35). The only explanation for the virgin birth is that it was a miracle performed by God. The Scriptures do not try to prove or explain how the virgin birth took place. It is written down as a fact and the implication is that without it there could be no salvation or redemption for sinful, fallen mankind. If Christ were not born of a virgin, then he would have been born 'in sin' like any other man, and therefore would have been unable to be the spotless sacrifice for the sins of the world (1 Peter 1:19). So every believer should praise God that His Son was born of a virgin and became "the Lamb of God, which taketh away the sin of the world" (John 1:29).

As Isaac's birth was a miracle, so is the new birth in Christ which every believer in the Lord Jesus experiences. Every person who has simply trusted the Lord Jesus for salvation has been miraculously born again by the Spirit of God (John 3). We call this regeneration. Through faith in God's Son, believers are given a new birth, a new life and are sealed unto God by the indwelling Holy Spirit (Ephesians 1:13; Romans 8:9). Therefore, the Apostle Paul could write: "And because ye are sons, God hath sent forth the Spirit of His Son into your hearts crying: Abba, Father" (Galatians 4:6). We also recall that as Isaac's birth caused joy and laughter, so each one who repents and believes on the Lord Jesus brings joy to the heart of God and to the multitude in Heaven, " . . . there is joy in the presence of the angels of God over one sinner that repenteth" (Luke 15:10).

We can imagine the unbridled joy in Abraham, Sarah and all their servants at the birth of Isaac. No doubt the servants were fully conversant with Abraham's faith in God. They had surely heard that God had promised a son by Sarah. Maybe some of them had shaken their heads in unbelief, possibly others had laughed behind their master's back. There was good reason for them to have been incredulous because Sarah was old and had been persistently barren. Yet on the birth of Isaac the whole household would have been filled with excitement and happiness, and a festive air would have come upon all, giving testimony to the faithfulness of God and Abraham's trust in Him. Later, a celebration was held, at the time of Isaac's weaning, possibly when he was as old as two or three years of age. In marking the occasion Abraham threw a "great feast" (Genesis 21:8). With such joyous festivities no wonder he was named Isaac.

In the meantime, at the tender age of eight days, Isaac was circumcised (Genesis 21:4). Here Abraham, as a true servant of God, was obeying the commandment of the Lord: "And he that is eight days old shall be circumcised among you, every man child in your generations, he that is born in the house, or bought with money of any stranger, which is not of thy seed" (Genesis 17:12). Abraham unquestioningly obeyed God. "To obey is better than sacrifice, and to hearken than the fat of rams" (1 Samuel 15:22). Likewise, the Christian's first response should not be to question God but to obey. It is easy to revert to selfishness, and not let Christ take full control of us. We will come to know the full blessing of God upon us, as we give Him our unquestioning obedience.

Yet why circumcise Isaac on the eighth day? Abraham did not choose the eighth day: God, the creator of all that is, instructed him to circumcise on the eighth day. It was only in 1929 that God allowed medical science to uncover the reason for the eighth day. In that year the existence in the human body of vitamin K was first suspected; it was soon isolated and has been widely used since 1939. One of its main uses is to help new born infants, often low in blood clotting ability, to have a healthy start in life. It appears that new born infants are prone to bleeding especially between the second and fifth days of life. This is partly due to the fact that the blood clotting factor vitamin K is insufficient in the bloodstream until the seventh day of life. There is also another blood clotting factor called prothrombin. On the third day of a baby's life this factor is only 30% of normal. However, on the eighth day it climbs to its one and only peak, to a level even higher than normal: 110%. After the eighth day it levels off to 100% for the rest of life, and so, on the eighth day a baby has more prothrombin available than on any other day of its whole life. The eighth day is thus the best day for an operation like circumcision. Clearly God knew all this, and man with the wonder of medical science confirms the accuracy of the Scriptures more than 4,000 years later.

Here we have a small indication of the truth that "all scripture is given by inspiration of God" (2 Timothy 3:16). In a small yet dramatic way we have a glimpse of the greatness of God and especially His omniscience. He is all-knowing. He must be, for He made everything (Genesis 1). We can take comfort and assurance in the trustworthiness of the Bible, God's Word. It is a book with a message, a message about redemption—that God's Son came into the world and died on the cross to redeem fallen mankind from sin. It is a book with a message to be believed. Let us believe it, and live by its precepts, for the Bible contains God's final and complete revelation to man.

The rite of circumcision for the Jewish nation was initiated when God commanded Abraham and his male descendants and dependants to be circumcised (Genesis 17:12). Circumcision was for a sign of the covenant relationship between God and His people. Stephen said: "And he gave him the covenant of circumcision: and so Abraham begat Isaac and circumcised him the eighth day..." (Acts 7:8). Thus it was the sign, a physical sign in their own bodies, that they had a covenant relationship with God. It was the removal of a part of their bodies which could harbour dirt and disease. Thus the possibility of infection was greatly reduced by circumcision. This would point to the moral implications of circumcision. The children of Israel had to live circumcised lives, that is lives where sin in its many manifestations would not be present. "And the Lord thy God will circumcise thine heart, and the heart of thy seed, to love the Lord thy God with all thine heart, and with all thy soul, that thou mayest live" (Deuteronomy 30:6).

Unfortunately, the children of Israel failed and did not always live lives of circumcision. They frequently forgot and forsook their covenant relationship with God, and went after idols and the sins associated with heathendom. Often this led to oppression by foreign invaders (see the book of Judges), deportation, slavery and exile. These were the consequences of breaking the covenant of circumcision. Stephen confirms the constant breaking of the covenant by the children of Israel: "Ye stiff-necked and uncircumcised in heart and ears, ye do always resist the Holy Ghost: as your fathers did, so do ye. Which of the prophets have not your fathers persecuted? And they have slain them which showed before of the coming of the Just One; of whom ye have been now the betrayers and murderers;" (Acts 7:51-52).

In the time in which we live, the dispensation of grace, God takes no account of the ordinance performed in the flesh—circumcision. The sole criterion for acceptance with God is faith in Christ. "In whom also ye are circumcised with the circumcision made without hands, in putting off the body of the sins of the flesh by the circumcision of Christ" (Colossians 2:11). "Circumcision is nothing, and uncircumcision is nothing, but the keeping of the commandments of God" (1 Corinthians 7:19). It is of great importance that believers keep His commandments. The Lord Jesus said: "If ye love me, keep my commandments" (John 14:15). When we keep His commandments we show that we belong to Him and that we are circumcised in heart. Some of His commandments are: to love one another (John 15:12), to witness wherever we go (Matthew 28:19), to remember Him in His death by breaking bread and drinking wine (1 Corinthians 11:23-29), to do good and keep our lives clean (James 1:27), to pray (1 Thessalonians 5:17) and to show hospitality (Hebrews 13:2). It is so important that: "Whatsoever he saith unto you, do it" (John 2:5).

So Isaac was circumcised at the age of eight days, in accordance with the covenant made between the Lord and Abraham. As the son of Sarah, he was the son of promise and he inherited all the wealth of Abraham, "And Abraham gave all that he had unto Isaac" (Genesis 25:5). He was also invested with the future promised blessings of a land and a people, and the spiritual promise: "in thy seed shall all the nations of the earth be blessed". These promises which had been given originally to Abraham, were renewed to Isaac (Genesis 26:3-5).

2. The Passive Life

There is little doubt that Isaac had a retiring, contemplative, yet affectionate nature. He was a man who avoided confrontations at all costs, and thus we could never imagine Isaac imitating Abraham's decisive action of arming his servants and overtaking the enemy in battle to rescue Lot (Genesis 14:13-24). Isaac lacked that outgoing forceful disposition. He would rather passively retreat than confront; would rather meditate than fight.

We see this very clearly in the incident recorded for us in Genesis 22. There Abraham was called upon by God to go to Mount Moriah and offer up Isaac as a human sacrifice. Abraham obeyed, but Isaac also was willing. He raised no objection to the desire of Abraham to obey God. This is remarkable for Isaac was not a little boy at that time. Josephus, the ancient historian, says that Isaac was twenty five years old at that time, while other commentators have suggested that he may have been as old as thirty or forty. So, clearly, he was an adult and as such could have objected most strongly to the whole plan. However, he did not, he submissively acceded to Abraham's binding cords and altar. He saw the knife poised in the hand of his father, with all its instant destructiveness and maybe too he heard the voice of God saying: "Abraham, Abraham" (Genesis 22:11). We might just wonder how much father and son had discussed the incident on their walk from the servants to the mount. Had Abraham told the whole story and the need to obey God totally? Had he told him of his faith that even though Isaac be slain, God could raise him to life again? (Hebrews 11:19). Whatever had been said, it is obvious that Isaac accepted his father's faith and desire to obey God. His faith may have been passive rather than active, yet there was no holding back, no grumbling, no complaining, only a willingness to be the sacrifice which God desired.

Again we see Isaac as a type of Christ. In a small way he mirrors the supreme sacrifice of all time. In Christ we see the fulfilment of that statement which Abraham gave to Isaac on the way to Mount Moriah: "My son, God will provide himself a lamb for a burnt offering . . . " (Genesis 22:8). John the Baptist on seeing the Lord Jesus said: "Behold the Lamb of God which taketh away the sin of the world" (John 1:29). Christ was willing to shed His blood and be slain for the sin of the whole world. So the picture of willing, submissive Isaac gives place to the greater reality of the willing, submissive Son of God. Isaac however was spared and was not slain. Christ was not spared and had to take the whole judgment of God and face it to the bitter end, so that there could be redemption for mankind. As we view the best which God gave us—His only Son—are we willing, like Isaac, to sacrifice all for Him? There are three sacrifices which we can and should be offering to the Lord.

Firstly, we must present our bodies to Him. "I beseech you therefore, brethren, by the mercies of God, that ye present your bodies a living **sacrifice**, holy, acceptable unto God, which is your reasonable service" (Romans 12:1). Here we are exhorted as Christians to yield our bodies to God, to let Him take full possession, to let Christ rise up and be supreme in our lives. In the Old Testament, the sacrifices on altars were slain—they were dead sacrifices—but we are to be living sacrifices.

Each day we need to renew our desire to let Christ have the place of lordship in our lives.

Secondly, we need to offer the sacrifice of praise. "By him therefore let us offer the **sacrifice** of praise to God continually, that is, the fruit of our lips giving thanks to His name" (Hebrews 13:15). This stems naturally from the first sacrifice, for if our bodies are completely yielded up to Him, it will include our lips and therefore what we say. Also as the first sacrifice is continual, so our praise to God should not restrict itself to the few hours each week which we spend meeting with fellow believers. We should not be like the children of Israel in the wilderness—murmuring and complaining—but should be characterised by continual praise and thanksgiving to the Lord.

Thirdly, we must make sacrifices in the area of financial and material giving. "But to do good and to communicate forget not; for with such **sacrifices** God is well pleased" (Hebrews 13:16). "I am full, having received of Epaphroditus the things which were sent from you, an odour of a sweet smell, a **sacrifice** acceptable, wellpleasing to God" (Philippians 4:18). All our financial giving should involve a measure of sacrifice. Like the widow who gave two mites, she gave until it hurt, for she gave all that she had (Mark 12:41-44).

In passive, unquestioning obedience we need to give ourselves and all that we have sacrificially to the Lord. Let us make the following our prayer:

> "Father I am willing to dedicate to thee,
> Life and talent, time and money,
> Here am I, send me".

Isaac further revealed his passive nature in straight-forwardly accepting Rebekah as his wife (Genesis 24:67). It is a beautiful story. We can imagine Isaac still sensing the loss of his mother, meditating in the fields and then looking up he saw the camel train return. The lovely Rebekah had been brought as a wife for Isaac, all the way from Haran by the old faithful servant of Abraham (Genesis 24). Isaac did not choose his wife, he accepted the choice of others. Yet he must have accepted the principle laid down by Abraham that he should not marry from the surrounding heathen nations. So he received Rebekah as his wife and installed her in his mother's tent where she took up the position formerly occupied by Sarah of leading lady in the family and household. Isaac was married at the age of forty (Genesis 25:20), and he not only accepted Rebekah but 'he loved her' and remained faithful to her all his life.

Yet the marriage had its fair share of problems. Initially, Rebekah was barren and that caused difficulties. Then after twenty years she had twins and they became the cause of further problems. Esau the elder was Isaac's favourite, Rebekah preferred Jacob (Genesis 25:28). Thus the boys who should have been a source of happiness and unity to Isaac and Rebekah became instead a source of friction and division. This led to Rebekah's scheme: she told Jacob to deceive the blind and ageing Isaac into giving the blessing to him and not to his older brother Esau (Genesis 27). Rebekah's scheme worked well. Jacob dressing in Esau's clothes smelt like Esau, with skins on his hands and neck he felt like hairy Esau, while the food which he carried in (cooked by Rebekah) tasted to Isaac just like that made by Esau. Only the voice was different and Isaac realised it, but he chose to believe the three senses rather than the one. His sight the fifth sense had failed. Thus Jacob received the patriarchal blessing and he followed Isaac in the line of promise instead of Esau.

This is a sad picture with Rebekah and Jacob deceiving Isaac to receive the Lord's blessing. Surely Isaac should have known the Lord's will anyway, or at least sought it through much labour in prayer. But no, his passive nature which had so wonderfully accepted Rebekah as bride years before, now caused him to take to his bed and to be idle in spiritual matters. He preferred Esau simply because Esau fed him and pampered to his fleshly appetite (Genesis 25:28). Yet Isaac is commended for his faith: "By faith, Isaac blessed Jacob and Esau concerning things to come" (Hebrews 11:20). He is commended because right at the end of his life his latent faith came to the surface to speak of future blessings to both sons, the greater blessing to Jacob, and the lesser to Esau. His faith was discerning enough to realise that in spite of Jacob's deception, this was the Lord's doing.

We can learn so much. Firstly, a husband and wife need to keep on building up their relationship. They need to work at communication with each other and never allow anyone (not even their children) to be a means of spoiling that relationship. The best relationship is when there is a spiritual dimension, when the marriage is in the Lord. Only then can it really develop and blossom into all its joyful fullness.

We must also never become self indulgent or flesh indulgent. Laziness and voluntary idleness are bad traits and need to be abhorred, particularly in the Lord's people. We are called upon to work and to serve the Lord. We are called upon to labour in the Lord's work. This labour is in prayer, preaching the Gospel, teaching spiritual truths to old and young and also the physical work of building, repairing and decorating the place where we meet for worship. There is no retirement or 'taking to our beds' in the service of the Master.

Isaac is also remembered for digging wells. Specifically, he dug again the wells which his father Abraham had dug (Genesis 26:18). Twice Isaac dug wells and on both occasions the Philistines contended with him for those wells. He gave them up, removed himself from the places of strife and dug again. This time the Philistines left him in peace. We could not imagine either Abraham or Jacob giving up what they had just worked for, but Isaac did just that.

It is of interest to note that Isaac had to re-dig his father's wells. With the passing of time they had been infilled and Isaac could not rely on what his father had done, he had to do it himself. He had to dig through the stones, rubble and rubbish to find the pure, refreshing water, which had previously been of sustenance to Abraham. Is it not true that we may have to cut through the unedifying traditions of men to experience the soul refreshing water of God's Word for ourselves? We may have to re-dig the wells which our forefathers dug. We cannot rely upon their experience, but need to know it first hand for ourselves. In other words we cannot live off the experience of previous generations. Every generation needs to know the Lord for itself. We need to dig the wells for ourselves, and then the blessing of the soul-cleansing water of God's Word can be ours.

Isaac's nature may have been passive, but he revealed

a deep and genuine faith in God. He is commended for his faith, even if it lacked the adventure and initiative that others showed. There is thus still much blessing for the quiet soul and much work which that person can do for the Lord. We each have work to do for the Master and it is important that we do it.

3. The Prayer Life

"And Isaac went out to meditate in the field at eventide ... " (Genesis 24:63)

"And Isaac intreated the Lord for his wife, because she was barren ... " (Genesis 25:21).

Isaac seems to have been greatly influenced by the actions and activities of Abraham, for he did many things which his father had done before him. As we have already seen Isaac re-dug the wells of his father (Genesis 26:17-22). Like his father he had to endure a famine in Canaan (Genesis 26:1-5), and it seems that he wanted to go down into Egypt for food; but the Lord prevented him from leaving Canaan. Both Abraham and Jacob spent time in Egypt, but not Isaac: maybe he was too weak a person for such an experience and so God did not allow it. Also like Abraham, Isaac used the plan of deceit, claiming Rebekah as his sister to escape possible death at the hands of the Philistines (Genesis 26:6-16). Unlike Abraham, however, this plan of deceit contained no element of truth, for Rebekah was a cousin and in no way a sister. Yet Isaac, like his father, also became very rich and was mightily blessed by the Lord. "Then Isaac sowed in that land, and received in the same year an hundredfold: and the Lord blessed him. And the man waxed great, and went forward, and grew until he became very great: for he had possession of flocks, and possession of herds, and great store of servants: and the Philistines envied him" (Genesis 26:12-14). This led the Philistines under Abimelech to seek a covenant of peace with Isaac as they had done previously with Abraham (Genesis 26:26-33). In all these ways Isaac followed in his father's footsteps.

But of more importance is the fact that he also manifested his father's faith, as well as his practices of sacrifice and prayer unto God, for Isaac built his own altar (Genesis 26:25) and spent time in meditation and prayer. In Genesis 24, Isaac is seen as a lonely figure, out in the field with no human companion. Maybe he was still grieving over the death of his mother a year or two before. We can imagine him walking along quietly talking to himself, no doubt also talking and communing with God. Alone in the creation communing with God is a wonderful way to find spiritual refreshment. I grew up in the mountains of South Wales and many times I walked alone in those hills and woods and was able to meditate upon the things of God. It was an uplift for both soul and spirit to walk in God's creation and spend time talking with Him. Such times produced invaluable spiritual blessings for me.

It may not be possible for all of us to enjoy the pleasures of the countryside as we meditate alone with God, but each Christian needs to develop a time of being alone with the Lord. This is a time when we centre our attention upon the Word of God and talk to the Father in prayer. Every believer should cultivate this daily habit, which we call the quiet time, as it is an intimate time of drawing close to the Lord. We need this regular spiritual refreshment for healthy Christian lives, so that we can bear fruit for God (Galatians

5:22-23). In Psalm 1 we read of a man who is described as blessed and verse 3 of the Psalm tells us that he is fruitful. His secret was that his delight was in the law of the Lord and in His law he meditated day and night (Psalm 1:2). If there is a barrenness in your spiritual life, then you might have to take a close look at this aspect of your life. Are you knowing the joy and blessing of a genuine quiet time with the Lord?

It would seem that mornings and evenings are the best time for most Christians to enjoy their quiet times. These are the occasions when the day's responsibilities have not yet started or else have ceased. We remember that the Lord Jesus got up early in the morning to pray: "And in the morning, rising up a great while before day, he went out, and departed into a solitary place, and there prayed" (Mark 1:35). He also prayed in the evening: " . . . he went out into a mountain to pray, and continued all night in prayer to God" (Luke 6:12). It is good for each believer to set aside such times for quietly drawing close to God. I know that this requires discipline. It might involve getting up earlier, or leaving the comfort of the armchair for a while, but the spiritual benefits make the effort well worthwhile.

The following is a suggested way of conducting the quiet time. It is intended for the young Christian, and is purely suggestive and must not be followed in any slavish fashion. It would be wise to choose a book of the Bible that is neither too long nor too involved e.g. the Gospel of Mark or the Gospel of John. Each day choose a paragraph (a chapter may prove too long and bring discouragement) to read in the quiet time. After an initial prayer to the Lord for help and understanding, read the verses very carefully two or three times, and then write down any meaningful thoughts or particular blessings which you may gain. Finally spend a few minutes in prayer. This need not, indeed must not, be simply a catalogue of requests, but should also include thanksgiving and praise. The time taken for the quiet time will vary according to individual concentration spans, but initially it should be at least 10 to 15 minutes. By attending diligently and faithfully to your quiet time, you will build up a bank of spiritual understanding, will gain much Christian blessing and will know a close communion with the Lord in daily life. This is the basis for a life of service for the Lord Jesus.

Isaac was a man of meditation, but he was also a man of intercession. In other words he let his "requests be made known unto God" (Philippians 4:6). For twenty years Isaac and Rebekah had failed to have any children, and so Isaac came before the Lord in intercessory prayer. He prayed in all earnestness for Rebekah. He prayed for her womb to be opened, for her barrenness to cease. He intreated the Lord, "and the Lord was intreated of him" (Genesis 25:21). The Lord heard his prayer and gave not simply one son, but two—twins, named Esau and Jacob. He asked and it was given unto him, and we can also come to the Lord and ask Him. Yet too often it might be true of us: " . . . ye have not, because ye ask not" (James 4:2).

In nineteenth century Bristol that great man of God, George Muller, cared for hundreds of orphans. It took a great deal of money to keep so many boys and girls in his care, yet he never resorted to publicity campaigns, begging letters or fund raising plans. He simply asked the Lord for food, for money, for staff, for clothing or whatever was the need of the hour. He intreated the

Lord and the Lord was intreated of him; and God still shows His power as the work amongst needy families in Bristol continues to this day.

The story is told of a preacher who went to a college in Oxford to minister to some of the students. As he spoke he felt a tremendous spiritual uplift from this group of Christians, and determined to find out the reason. In the informal session afterwards he talked to the students individually, and discovered that six months previously two students had spent a night in prayer. They had intreated the Lord to help them lead one person to Christ. The Lord was intreated of them and in the subsequent months He had not only given them one convert, but fifty or sixty beside.

This should challenge our hearts to be people who intreat the Lord. All too often we want blessing, but are not prepared to spend the time asking for it. Yet the Lord says to us: "Ask and it shall be given unto you ... " (Matthew 7:7) and " ... whatsoever ye shall ask in my name that will I do, that the Father may be glorified in the Son" (John 14:13).

Isaac's prayer life seems to have influenced Rebekah, for she went herself to enquire of the Lord the meaning of the struggle in her womb. God, in response to her prayer, gave her a glimpse of the future. She would have two sons and they would become two nations (these were subsequently Edom and Israel). God also revealed to her that one would be stronger than the other: " ... the elder shall serve the younger" (Genesis 25:23). So prayer was an important feature in the lives of Isaac and Rebekah. Sadly it does not appear to have continued, as Isaac resorted to his bed and Rebekah to deceit. Let us however be praying, interceding believers, with no thought of giving up, constantly before the throne of grace. Let us be continually praying for an extension to His kingdom and for His name to be glorified, exalted and magnified.

"...men ought always to pray, and not to faint" (Luke 18:1).

"And let us not be weary in well doing: for in due season we shall reap, if we faint not" (Galatians 6:9).